THE WESTERN REGION IN THE 1970S AND 1980S

Andy Gibbs

AMBERLEY

Front Cover above: Waiting to depart Exeter St Davids with a service to Waterloo, No. 50013 *Agincourt* simmers in the platform. 4 May 1987. (M. Hull)

Front Cover below: No. 47662 exits Dainton tunnel with what is probably the southbound Cornish Scot. 31 May 1989.

Back cover: Accelerating through Teignmouth, No. 46046 heads east with 1E37, the 10.53 Paignton to Leeds cross-country service. 12 April 1980.

First published 2018

Amberley Publishing
The Hill, Stroud
Gloucestershire, GL5 4EP

www.amberley-books.com

Copyright © Andy Gibbs, 2018

The right of Andy Gibbs to be identified as the Author of this work has been asserted in accordance with the Copyrights, Designs and Patents Act 1988.

ISBN 978 1 4456 8177 1 (print)
ISBN 978 1 4456 8178 8 (ebook)

British Library Cataloguing in Publication Data.
A catalogue record for this book is available from the British Library.

Origination by Amberley Publishing.
Printed in the UK.

Introduction

A bit like the recording artist's 'difficult second album', welcome to my difficult second book, the first one being for the Southern Region. This book has taken longer than I expected, with the extra time being used taken to pick and choose the locations and photographs. I hope you enjoy the journey.

Other than London, getting off the Southern Region from my home in Brighton meant you were Western-bound. To get in a decent day's trainspotting meant either a very early start and off to Reading via Redhill and the never-ending journey on a Tadpole unit, or to Westbury via Portsmouth, extending the use on a Southern runabout ticket. Summer Saturdays meant that the West Country and Bristol was reachable on a direct train and much time was spent at Bristol, and later a full day on the sea wall at Dawlish.

On trips to London, other than Marylebone, Paddington was probably the London terminal station I visited least. Euston, St Pancras and King's Cross were favourites as they were so close together.

Later holidays and trips with my Student Railcard took me to South Wales, and once I started working for British Rail the free pass was definitely a ticket to ride.

A good constitution was required, with meals being mainly a sandwich from the train or station buffet and a packet of racy Big D peanuts washed down with McEwan's Export and a Lyons apple pie. Those were the days!

This is a record of my trips and those of others in the 1970s and '80s throughout the Western Region when British Rail was blue and grey, brake-dust coloured and a great place to work.

We start our journey on the Western Region, ironically with a Southern DEMU. The ASLEF strikes of 1982 saw some unusual workings when any trains ran. At Paddington we find 3D unit No. 1319, having arrived earlier from Basingstoke, taken between 5 July and 18 July 1982. (A. Edwards)

It's going to be a stuffy journey today as No. No. 47227, fitted with steam heat only, departs from Paddington with an unidentified InterCity service on 12 May 1983.

No. 47056 arrives at Paddington station on a lovely sunny day with an unidentified service. September 1979.

With over forty years' service under their belts, the HSTs are a classic design still working front-line InterCity services today. At Paddington on 25 July 1981 we find sets Nos 253029, 019 and 014 lined up ready for their next services. (J. A. Lower)

This atmospheric image at Paddington has No. 47582 *County of Norfolk* on the wrong side of London with a parcels train. BRUTE trolleys line the platform. The loco had recently been re-allocated from Stratford to Old Oak Common. November 1987.

Class 31s were synonymous with the ECS workings at Paddington and here we find No. 31412 waiting to depart for Old Oak Common. 25 July 1981. (J. A. Lower)

Westbourne Park and with the Westway traffic roaring overhead, HST set No. 253043 heads away from Paddington while a pair of Class 33s with an aggregates train wait in the adjacent sidings.

At Old Oak Common the West London line dropped down from its elevated route at North Pole Junction to join the route out of Paddington. Here we find an unidentified Class 47 passing the signal box while working 1M50, the 08.47 Brighton to Manchester Piccadilly cross-country service. July 1983.

Thundering towards the photographer at Acton Main Line is No. 50031 *Hood* with a 'Thames Valley' service formed mainly of NSE-liveried Mk 2 stock. March 1989.

Arriving at Ealing Broadway is Class 117 DMU set No. L424 on a Paddington to Reading service. The L designated a London-allocated set. The other letters used were B for Bristol, C for Cardiff and P for Plymouth. 23 August 1986.

Large Logo-liveried No. 47813 passes through Southall station with 1O99, the 06.18 Manchester Piccadilly to Folkestone Central. By 1989 this was now the sole InterCity cross-London service running into Kent. August 1989.

On an overcast day, Class 50 No. 50018 *Resolution* has charge of a Paddington to Oxford service, and is seen here at Taplow. August 1986.

Hoover superpower for this Thames Valley service as No. 50042 *Triumph* pilots a sister loco through Taplow.
September 1988.

A little further west at Ruscombe we find No. 47240 working a long train of 45-ton tank wagons toward
London on the Up relief line. 29 June 1981.

Heading towards London we find No. 47267 in charge of a long van train, the first three being Syphon Gs. The train is captured at Twyford. 29 July 1980.

With exhaust billowing, No. 47097 is working hard at Twyford with a heavy eastbound tank train, which includes a barrier wagon. 29 July 1980.

Heading west at Ruscombe near Twyford with an eight-car ECS is Landore-allocated No. 47157. The loco sported the unusual two white discs painted on the cab end during the early 1980s. 29 July 1983.

No. 47226 is caught trundling along the Down relief line at Ruscombe with a long vacuum-braked train formed mainly of empty coal hoppers, although a permanent way wagon and some 21-ton open wagons can also be seen. 30 June 1981.

Entering Sonning cutting with an air-braked freight train formed of a five-car container set and a pair of Cartic 4 car transporters is Cardiff-allocated No. 47238. 26 March 1980.

A fine image of No. 47298 in Sonning cutting with a freight train. The first wagon is in permanent way service, carrying some cable drums, and is followed by a ferry van. 14 May 1979.

On the Up relief in Sonning cutting we find Cardiff Canton-allocated No. 47258 with a long van train. Five Syphon Gs are separated by a former LMS vehicle. 9 August 1977.

A lovely summer's day and the driver of No. 50002 *Superb* is hanging well out of the cab window to get the 'tip' from the conductor at Twyford station. The service is on the Down relief line. June 1986.

Landore-allocated No. 47068 is working hard on the Up relief line at Sonning with a loaded train of Polybulk hoppers filled with China clay, bound for the train ferry at Dover for onward transit to Switzerland. 20 March 1980.

Ex-works No. 73104 doesn't appear to contributing much while double-heading No. 33028 on this long container train captured near Sonning. 23 September 1980.

Probably the best looking of the DMU classes, Swindon-built InterCity Class 123 DMU set No. L714 stands at Reading while working a train towards Oxford. April 1973.

4VEP No. 7752 and a sister unit arrive at Reading with a train from Waterloo.

Approaching Reading station while heading back to the West Country is No. 31309 with a train of empty milk tanks. 1975.

On a grim winter's day No. 47076 *City of Truro* passes through Reading with a train of carflats loaded with Ford Transit chassis cabs and vans. In the adjacent siding is a Matisa Neptune track recording trolley. October 1975. (A. Gibbs)

With the driver leaning out of the cab for the 'right away', Hoover No. 50035 waits to depart from Reading with an InterCity service for Paddington. The loco was later named *Ark Royal*. October 1975. (A. Gibbs)

No. 50005 departs Reading station with a westbound InterCity service. The platform end in the foreground had no track on the far side and was regularly used as a seat by the numerous trainspotters here. The loco was later named *Collingwood*. October 1975. (A. Gibbs)

A busy scene at Reading as Nos 33104 and 33011 depart with a train from the Midlands to Poole. On the adjacent track are Nos 47078 *Sir Daniel Gooch* and 08799. August 1977. (J. A. Lower)

Crewe-allocated No. 47345 is laying down some serious clag as it approaches Reading with a long train of bogie Presflo cement hoppers. The lines in the foreground are the Southern route towards Waterloo. 1976.

14 May 1979 saw the start of direct services from Brighton to Manchester Piccadilly via the West London line and the Thames Valley. It didn't take me long to get a trip on the morning service to Reading. Here we see No. 47459 about to depart with 1M50, the 09.07 from Brighton to Manchester. The ride in the Mk 1 compartment coach was a vast improvement on the DEMU from Redhill. May 1979. (A. Gibbs)

Problems with the HST power cars saw a set of Mk 3 trailers being paired up with a Mk 1 generator van and loco-hauled between Bristol Temple Meads and London. At Reading we find No. 47095 slowing for the station stop. November 1980. (A. Gibbs)

What No. 40024 *Lucania* is doing at Reading I have no idea. The loco is seen here running light towards London. The nameplates were removed in 1973 and the loco is sporting some hand-painted ones. The offside nose-end handrail looks like it's been in the wars. November 1980. (A. Gibbs)

With a motley selection of wagons in tow, No. 47327 trundles through Reading as it heads towards London. 23 April 1981.

4VEP No. 7759 has recently arrived from Waterloo as No. 47512 waits to depart Reading with 1O74, the 07.30 Manchester Piccadilly to Brighton service, the InterCity service having a mixture of Mk 1 and different Mk 2 types of coaches. 23 February 1983.

An unusual view of the western end of Reading station, taken from Thames Tower. An unidentified 3H DEMU arrives on a service from Basingstoke. The landmark building of the training tower at the fire station can easily be identified. 20 July 1983.

It was rare of me to take photographs of coaches, but I made an exception in this case. No. RDB977091 was an attempt by BR to breathe new life into the huge fleet of Mk 1 coaches. Built using Leyland National bus parts and mounted on the chassis of the former BCK No. M21234, it was to be a one-off, but partly spawned the Pacer DMU. Inside it was bright and airy with standard road coach seats; the internal panels were very similar to the nicotine-coloured ones that were later fitted to the Pacers. The coach is seen here in the formation of 1M50, the 08.47 Brighton to Manchester Piccadilly. November 1983. (A. Gibbs)

Sneaking through the centre road at Reading while an HST performs its station stop, No. 47246 has a short train of bogie Presflo hoppers in tow. 4 May 1985. (G. Edwards)

The SR were very good at temporary unit reformations and here we see an example. 6L Motor Brake Second No. S60022 from unit No. 1015, still sporting 1066 line branding, which had been disbanded, is found forming 3H unit No. 1107 at Reading. The trailer cars from unit No. 1015 ended up in unit No. 1003 with the other MBSs being scrapped. March 1986.

Not much happening, lads – the east end of Reading station on a hot summer's day and a very different view to the present day. A 4CIG waits to depart from the Southern bays for Waterloo and a Class 117 DMU waits to return to Paddington. It may be time for a Lyons apple pie from the Travellers Fare buffet. 4 August 1976.

Class 50 No. 50015 *Valiant* approaches Reading with a Down Thames Valley service. The gasometers remain a prominent feature at Reading even now. July 1986.

Rounding the corner at Reading West, No. 47257 trundles through with a permanent way train. 12 February 1981.

We resume our journey down the Thames Valley. With the locomotive and front set of doors off the platform at Tilehurst, the driver of No. 47033 looks back down the train for the signal from the guard to depart. 27 May 1982.

Container traffic to and from Southampton is a big business, which BR managed to hold on to. No. 47323 is captured near Goring with a well-loaded train. 12 April 1980.

Like many rail enthusiasts, Merrymaker excursions were a very cheap way of getting out and about for me. On this journey from the Sussex Coast to Oxford I managed to catch No. 47056 near Didcot while being propped up against the door droplight. 1976. (A. Gibbs)

Scurrying away from Didcot, with the power station in the background, No. 47236 is seen on the Up relief line with a train of 100-ton tank wagons. 3 April 1984. (M. Hull).

Making plenty of exhaust smoke as it works hard with a long loaded stone train, No. 47568 is captured south of Oxford with 6M24, the 06.40 Tytherington to Wolverton. 11 February 1988. (M. Hull).

While a Class 117 DMU is stabled in the sidings at Oxford, No. 47485 departs with 1O74, the 10.23 Manchester Piccadilly to Brighton. A single SSA scrap wagon and a mineral wagon can be seen in the yard. 31 August 1983.

Missing the 1 from the headcode, No. 47232 waits to depart from Oxford with 1C58, the 12.35 Paddington to Hereford. 10 May 1975.

Southbound at Oxford, we find No. 47341 waiting to depart with an unidentified train. 5 May 1982.

You could guarantee a stream of cross-country trains at Oxford with workings from the North East and the North West heading to and from the South Coast resorts. Here we find No. 47538 snaking into the platform, its train of Mk 1 coaches forming 1O27, the 06.45 York to Portsmouth Harbour. 29 August 1984.

The passengers on 1O92, the 13.56 Liverpool Lime Street to Portsmouth Harbour, have an unexpected bonus today as the train is largely formed of Mk 2 first class air-conditioned vehicles. The downside is that the motive power is No. 47197, so no ETH for the air conditioning. The combination gets away from Oxford. 29 August 1984.

Low winter sunlight highlights No. 47543 at Oxford as it waits to depart with 1O11, the 09.50 Glasgow Central to Poole 'Wessex Scot'. 18 February 1987.

No race here. In the platform waiting to depart with the 1650 Oxford to Paddington is HST set No. 253039 with power car No. 43147 leading. Nos 33019 and 33030 double-head a train of carflats, probably returning to the Ford transit factory at Eastleigh. 15 February 1983. (B. Watkins).

Car production has been associated with the Oxford area for a very long time, from Morris through British Leyland, Rover Cars and MG Rover to the BMW Mini. No. 47117 is captured on film with 4V16, the 09.35 Washwood Heath to Morris Cowley service. The formation is at Kidlington, on the outskirts of Oxford. 7 October 1986. (M. Hull)

Shipton Cement Works, just north of Oxford, finds No. 56056 hurrying south with a loaded coal train bound for Didcot Power Station. The cement works closed in 1986. 11 February 1981. (M. Hull)

Near Tackley, Oxon, we find No. 45120 with 1M14, the 13.07 Paddington to Liverpool Lime Street. The Peak would work the train as far as New Street. The loco would have normally arrived in the capital earlier that day on a service from Cardiff and would later work a Birmingham to Bristol service to return the engine west. 12 April 1984. (M. Hull)

Sweeping through the Oxfordshire countryside at Tackley, No. 47607 heads south with an unidentified cross-country service. 15 June 1984. (M. Hull)

No. 47212 trundles light engine through the lush countryside at Frampton Mansell, between Kemble and Stroud. 16 May 1987. (M. Hull)

Resuming our journey south-west from Reading we find Nos 37244 and 37257 with a train of empty Yeoman 'mashed potato' hoppers, waiting on signals at Newbury. A young group of trainspotters watch the lack of proceedings. 1982.

Until the direct train from Brighton to Bristol started running, Westbury was the limit of my expeditions westward – having got here from Brighton on a SR runabout ticket and a cheap day return student railcard from Salisbury. No. 47085, sans nameplates, waits to depart with empty hoppers on a damp spring day. 1975. (A. Gibbs)

A very busy scene at Westbury with, from left to right, No. 47094 (an HST set) and No. 33035 departing on 1V20, the 08.10 Portsmouth Harbour to Cardiff Central. Two more Class 47s can be seen in the background. 27 June 1985. (P. Barber)

No. 33056 *Burma Star* is captured at Westbury with 1V46, the 08.30 Brighton to Cardiff Central. 10 April 1987. (B. Hayes)

Approaching Westbury station is No. 33029 with 1O85, the 15.10 Cardiff Central to Brighton service. Despite the shabby Mk 1 coaches, the services always loaded well. 24 June 1987. (P. Barber)

The only Western I ever knowingly saw was D1022 *Western Sentinel* at Reading in the pouring rain, and the photographs I took of it are atrocious. To make up for that I have acquired a few images of the Westerns towards the ends of their working lives. At Westbury, amidst the forest of semaphore signals, we find D1021 *Western Cavalier* departing with an Up service from the West Country. April 1976.

An extremely neglected D1063 *Western Monitor* has a train of ventilated vans at Westbury. No Hi-Viz vests on this day! April 1976.

No. 47274 arrives at Castle Cary with a Penzance to Paddington working formed of Mk 1 stock. The station is looking very tidy. 12 April 1982. (G. Roose)

An unidentified Peak clears Cogload Junction with a westbound Motorail service. This is probably the Saturday-only Newcastle to Newton Abbot service, which also attached carflats at York and Sheffield. August 1979.

Standing alongside at Taunton station are Class 47s Nos 47198 and 47148, both with unidentified westbound services. 30 June 1979.

With an unusual variation of the former headcode box, No. 45019 restarts a Down freight train away from the yard at Silk Mills crossing, Taunton, with another load of Allegros and Minis for the West Country, plus some air-braked vans. 26 March 1980.

Near Bridgewater, No. 45075 is caught working 1V67, the 08.02 Saturdays-only Nottingham to Paignton service. 6 August 1983.

At Tiverton Junction we find push-pull Crompton No. 33108 with a train of 45-ton tank wagons from Fawley. Class 33s past Exeter were relatively rare at this time. 25 March 1976.

6L Hastings DEMU unit No. 1013 sits at Exeter St Davids, waiting to work the 13.55 Saturdays-only service through to Brighton. In the summer months, prior to reverting to a loco-hauled service, this train also conveyed a 6B buffet unit. April 1973.

At the north end of Exeter St Davids we find D1033 *Western Trooper* working an unidentified additional service. 18 July 1975.

Stabled alongside St Davids station are Class 31s Nos 31124 and 31135, both in an absolutely filthy condition. 15 July 1978.

Nos 47090 *Vulcan* and 33001 are found between duties alongside the signal box at Exeter St Davids. June 1981. (M. Howarth)

An unidentified Class 50 sits at Exeter St Davids, slowly filling the station with exhaust fumes. It is about to depart with 1O49, the 09.35 to Waterloo. March 1989.

Arriving at Exeter St Davids are Nos 33206 and 33049 with 1V71, the 09.20 Saturdays-only Brighton to Paignton. The two Cromptons and the adjacent buffet car will be detached here and then work back to Brighton on the 13.05 service from Paignton. 11 September 1982.

Passing Exeter Central signal box are pristine Nos 33043 and 33015 as they accelerate away from the station with 1O86, the 13.40 Saturdays-only Exeter St Davids to Brighton service. 8 August 1981.

Trains passing at Chard Junction: No. 50016 *Barham* is on an Exeter St Davids to Waterloo service, while the approaching No. 50006 *Neptune* is working a service from Waterloo to Exeter. 13 July 1986.

Crompton No. 33040 gets away from Yeovil Junction station with 1V10, the 09.13 Saturdays-only Brighton to Exeter St Davids. The winter timetable saw this service reduced to eight cars and a single locomotive. 11 October 1986.

Motorail trains are another sight that has disappeared from Britain's railways. At Dawlish Warren, an unidentified Class 47 rounds the curve with a long train, en route to St Austell. September 1976. (P. Geary)

At Dawlish we find an unidentified Class 47 with a string of Newton Chambers Mk 1 car carriers on the Newton Abbot to Sheffield Motorail service. Only fourteen of these were built and at least six can be seen on this train. Newton Chambers had a diverse portfolio of interests, as along with engineering they also made Izal toilet paper!

A pleasant autumn day in 1980 sees an unidentified HST set on the sea wall at Dawlish, heading for London. November 1980. (A. Edwards)

A year earlier, in October 1979, the waves are breaking over the sea wall as an unidentified train enters Kennaway Tunnel at Dawlish. (A. Edwards)

Back to autumn 1980 and an unidentified Class 47 makes light work of a six-coach train, working a local service from Exeter along the sea wall at Dawlish. A great selection of '70s cars can be seen. (A. Edwards)

July 1984 saw three of us board the Waterloo to Exeter overnight train for a day on the sea wall at Dawlish. Armed with a list of services gleaned from the CRS seat reservations system, we arrived in Dawlish in time for breakfast. We had a great day but the weather didn't play ball, being more like November than July. The next few images are from that day.

No. 45137 *Bedfordshire and Hertfordshire Regiment TA* heads a cross-country service towards Exeter. Some enthusiasts salute from the windows. 14 July 1984. (A. Gibbs)

Despite the cold and windy day, some are more hardy than others. No. 47279 passes by with the carflats loaded with cars on a Motorail service from Paddington. The passengers were conveyed on scheduled services by this time. 14 July 1984. (A. Gibbs)

You were always going to guarantee plenty of Peak action on this day, and this was a bonus. No. 45022 *Lytham St Annes* pilots an ailing HST set on the 13.36 Paignton to Newcastle service. 14 July 1984. (A. Gibbs)

No. 50045 *Achilles* gets a wave from holidaymakers as it heads east with 1S71, the 07.40 Penzance to Glasgow Central. The loco worked the train to Birmingham New Street. 14 July 1984. (A. Gibbs)

'My Lords'! Nos 46047 and 47188 double-head 1E32, the 16.45 Paignton to Leeds cross-country service. Both locos were working, with the 'Peak bashers' not remembering to not lean out of the window! Great times. 14 July 1984. (A. Gibbs)

Also heading west is this unidentified Class 47 with a cross-country service. 14 July 1984. (A. Gibbs)

An usual view at Dawlish as a London-bound HST set pauses at the station. September 1984. (A. Edwards)

Bowling along the sea wall at Dawlish we find No. 33004, displaying a 62 headcode (Exeter to Waterloo) and what looks like the correct formation of coaches. The slide is dated June 1980 but there were no SR services booked past Exeter at this time, so this is a bit of a conundrum. Perhaps this was an ECS move from Newton Abbot or Laira?

No. 47513 *Severn* makes a fine sight as it accelerates away from the station stop at Dawlish. There are also some fine examples of British motoring in the car park. 23 July 1982.

Another unusual view of Dawlish station as No. 47463 leans into the curve with 1V12, the 11.05 Saturdays-only Brighton to Plymouth service. 27 August 1988.

Powering along the sea wall at Teignmouth, No. 47660, in Large Logo livery, makes light work of its six-coach train. 16 July 1989.

Caught in the telephoto lens is No. 46009, in charge of 1V71, the 06.56 Saturdays-only Bradford Exchange to Penzance service. A lone old lady watches from the sea wall at Teignmouth. 12 April 1980.

At Teignmouth No. 47435 is working 1V55, the 09.20 Liverpool Lime Street to Penzance. September 1986.

Still in two-tone green livery, No. 47256 pauses at Newton Abbot with an unidentified service. 9 May 1976.

One of my favourite photographs as drivers prepare their cars to be unloaded from a Motorail service at Newton Abbot. Seen here is a typical 1970s line-up of cars, including a Mk 3 Ford Cortina, an Austin/Morris 1100/1300, a Hillman Minx and a Vauxhall Victor. 18 August 1972.

Running parallel with the A380 at Aller Junction is No. 50024 *Vanguard* with 1V86, the 13.44 Saturdays-only Birmingham New Street to Paignton service. 23 June 1984.

No. 45045, named *Coldstream Guardsman*, rolls into Paignton station with an unidentified service. September 1979.

No. 45027, fitted with a split headcode box, passes through Totnes station with an unidentified cross-country service. 6 October 1976.

No. 47558 *Mayflower* is caught with a train of Mk 1 coaches near Totnes. July 1984. (P. Barber)

A deserted Plymouth station with No. 47216 on a van train. 5 May 1976.

There are plenty of trains in this view of Plymouth, with two passenger trains separated by No. 45074, which is heading a freight train. The leading wagon is an unidentified ferry van. 5 August 1981.

Having just arrived at Plymouth, No. 50030 *Repulse* rests after having worked there on 1V32, the 23.50 Glasgow to Plymouth. 12 March 1988.

St Budeaux Ferry Road station is where the branch line to Gunnislake parts company from the main line. Class 119 DMU set P588 waits to depart. Note Tavistock on the destination blind. Passenger services to Tavistock were withdrawn at the end of 1962! 17 June 1974. (C. Parker)

An unidentified Class 47 starts to cross the Saltash bridge with a permanent way train in tow. This unusual view is taken from Lower Fore Street in Saltash. October 1980. (A. Edwards)

An unidentified Peak has charge of a permanent way train when seen on Liskeard Viaduct. June 1985. (R. Siviter)

At Liskeard station we find an unidentified Western working 1B45, the 11.30 Paddington to Penzance. 14 June 1974. (C. Parker)

Curving off the Looe branch at Liskeard is a Swindon-built, cross-country DMU set, No. P554, allocated to Plymouth Laira depot. At this time the unit consisted of coaches Nos W51575, W59292 and W51584. 14 June 1974. (C. Parker)

Waiting to depart Liskeard with a westbound service is a Plymouth-allocated, Gloucester-built, cross-country Class 119 DMU, set No. P577. July 1976.

Near Par we find No. 47632 working an unidentified InterCity service. 22 April 1988. (M. Hull)

Its No. 47632 again, this time at Burngallow Junction as it sweeps by with 1S87, the 10.27 Penzance to Glasgow and Edinburgh 'Cornish Scot'. April 1988. (R. Siviter)

At the end of the branch line from St Erth we find a two-car DMU formed of Class 118 vehicles, waiting at St Ives for the return journey to St Erth. October 1983.

At the end of the line we find HST set No. 253037, which is waiting to form a service back to London from Penzance. 3 September 1981.

We now retrace our steps from Cornwall to Swindon and will head west towards Bristol and South Wales.

A gloomy day finds No. 47487 in InterCity livery with a van train at Swindon. 9 March 1986.

Passing Freshford station is No. 33016, which is on a service from Bristol Temple Meads to Portsmouth. April 1988.

Powering through the S bends at Limpley Stoke, near Freshford, push-pull Crompton No. 33103 is working 1V46, the 08.30 Brighton to Cardiff Central service. 22 April 1988.

On a bright and misty winter morning at Claverton, just to the east of Bath, we find No. 33034 working 1V46, the 08.30 Brighton to Cardiff. 6 January 1987. (M. Hull)

With the low evening sun illuminating the train, No. 33029 coasts into Bath Spa station with 1V34, the 17.10 Portsmouth Harbour to Bristol Temple Meads service. 31 July 1984.

Departing from Bath Spa with a Portsmouth Harbour to Cardiff Central service is No. 33016. 13 May 1980.

No. 47234 has arrived at Bath Spa with 1M26, the 12.50 Saturdays-only Weymouth to Derby. This train was unusually routed via Yeovil Pen Mill and Bristol Temple Meads before heading north. 14 June 1975. (C. Parker)

A nice display of flowers at Bath Spa as No. 33002 arrives with 1O43, the 14.05 Cardiff Central to Portsmouth Harbour. 13 July 1986. (I. J. Stewart)

West of Bath, at Twerton Tunnel, No. 33029 has charge of a Portsmouth to Cardiff service.

Keynsham station and a lone passenger watches as No. 33015 works an unidentified Portsmouth Harbour to Cardiff Central service. 20 April 1988.

Once the direct train from Brighton to Bristol started running in 1979, this became another favourite destination for us. Plenty of trainspotters are here to witness a filthy No. 47131 rolling into Bristol Temple Meads with 1M39, the 09.32 Saturdays-only Penzance to Wolverhampton service. 19 July 1980. (A. Gibbs)

Nos 33009 and 33025 run into Temple Meads with an ECS train from Malago Vale, which will form 1O83, the 15.05 departure to Portsmouth Harbour. 19 July 1980. (A. Gibbs)

The WR didn't seem to bother with cleaning locos, as this unidentified Class 31/4 at Bristol can testify. Meanwhile, a pair of young trainspotters rest their legs, it being time for a sandwich. 1978. (J. A. Lower)

No. 45049 *The Staffordshire Regiment* pauses at Bristol Temple Meads with 1V42, the 08.39 Saturdays-only Manchester Piccadilly to Newquay service. 19 July 1980. (A. Gibbs)

A night-time scene at Bristol with No. 37173 assisting an unidentified, and probably failed, Class 47.

Finsbury Park-allocated No. 31406 has managed to slip the net as it gets away from Temple Meads with an unidentified North East to South West working. 19 July 1980. (A. Gibbs)

No. 47492 arrives at Bristol with an unidentified service from the West Country. 19 July 1980. (A. Gibbs)

Grey exhaust billows from No. 50030 *Repulse* as it waits to depart Bristol for Swansea with 1V54, the 10.10 from Portsmouth Harbour. 13 June 1987. (P. J. Fitton)

Peaks were the mainstay of the North East to South West route for many years. No. 45104 *The Royal Warwickshire Regiment* is working 1V89, the 12.23 Manchester Piccadilly to Paignton, when seen here at Temple Meads. 29 August 1981. (A. Gibbs)

A smart-looking No. 47500 *Great Western* rolls into Temple Meads with a parcels train. 19 July 1980. (A. Gibbs)

Grubby was the typical condition for most WR locomotives and here we find No. 47076 *City of Truro* at Bristol Temple Meads with an unidentified North East to South West working. 19 July 1980. (A. Gibbs)

Stabled between duties at Bristol Temple Meads is No. 33016. 30 July 1987. (M. Hull)

Accelerating away from Temple Meads station is Western Region No. 47079 *G. J. Churchward*, which is seen working 1C44, the 13.53 Paignton to Swansea. 29 August 1981. (A. Gibbs)

No. 33010 arrives at Bristol Temple Meads with a Cardiff to Portsmouth service. 29 August 1981. (A. Gibbs)

At the north end of Bristol Temple Meads, No. 33030 departs with a service bound for Cardiff Central. 29 August 1981. (A. Gibbs)

Waiting to depart for Malago Vale carriage sidings, No. 47152 has just arrived at Bristol Temple Meads with 1V27, the 12.15 from Portsmouth Harbour. 19 July 1980. (A. Gibbs)

Hoover No. 50040 *Leviathan* is working 1V76, the 13.22 Liverpool Lime Street to Plymouth service, when seen here at Bristol Temple Meads. 1 May 1982.

Class 45/0 No. 45037 waits to depart Bristol Temple Meads with 1M22, the 08.55 Penzance to Manchester Piccadilly. An HST set can be seen lurking in the depths of the train shed. 6 August 1983.

Push-pull-fitted Class 33 No. 33105 approaches Bristol Temple Meads with a service from Portsmouth Harbour. (J. R. Carter)

Back in the day there was also a small network of cross-country trains that included sleeping cars. At journey's end we find No. 45143 *5th Royal Inniskilling Dragoon Guards* with 1V61, the 22.55 Glasgow Central to Bristol Temple Meads. 13 August 1983.

No. 47203 still retains its two-tone green livery when spotted at Bristol Temple Meads with a North East to South West service. 3 August 1975.

Curving into Bristol Temple Meads, No. 47237 has a long train of empty Polybulk hoppers, which started their journey in Switzerland and are en route back to the St Austell area. August 1984.

Network SouthEast coaches and a non-boiler-fitted Class 47 at Bristol. No. 47308 departs with an unidentified service for the West Country. September 1986.

No. 45032 waits to depart Bristol Temple Meads with an unidentified North East to South West service. 19 July 1980. (A. Gibbs)

Just south of Temple Meads is Malago Vale carriage sidings, and here we find No. 33027 on a short parcels train consisting of just one SR and one BR CCT van. 4 July 1980.

Victoria Park, Bristol, and the W. D. & H. O. Wills cigarette factory dominates the skyline as No. 45046 works the ECS from Malago Vale into Temple Meads to form 1S61, the 08.20 departure to Glasgow Central. No. 47369, still in two-tone green livery, passes with the Glasgow to Bristol West Depot Freightliner service. July 1975.

Horton Road, Gloucester, and just No. 45039 *Manchester Regiment* is in the sidings. Summer 1975. (A. Gibbs)

It is a nice summer's day as No. 47523 arrives at Gloucester with a cross-country service. (A. Gibbs)

No. 47480 *Robin Hood* was always one of my favourite locos – I was even at its naming ceremony in Nottingham, in November 1979. At Gloucester we find the loco working 1M22, the 11.25 Plymouth to Manchester Piccadilly. 19 April 1980.

No. 47465 is captured at Cheltenham Spa with an unidentified northbound service. 29 August 1981. (A. Gibbs)

No. 45006 lays down a cloud of exhaust as it passes through Cheltenham Spa station with an unidentified North East to South West service. 29 August 1981. (A. Gibbs)

The west end of Seven Tunnel Junction and No. 33013 is en route to Cardiff Central with a service from Portsmouth Harbour. 10 September 1985.

At Abergavenny we find No. 47258 with a Bristol Temple Meads to Stirling Motorail service. This train was routed via Hereford. 19 September 1984.

Maindee Junction at Newport and No. 47625 *Vulcan* curves off the Hereford line with a service from Manchester Piccadilly. 5 April 1988. (M. Hull)

No. 33026 is seen at Maindee Junction, Newport, with a Portsmouth Harbour to Cardiff Central working.
5 April 1988. (M. Hull)

Approaching Newport is No. 47616 *Y Ddraig Goch/The Red Dragon* with an unidentified westbound service.
August 1986.

No. 37208 departs from Newport with 2B38, the 14.02 Cardiff Central to Bristol Temple Meads. 22 September 1983.

Fast forward four years from the previous image and No. 50018 *Resolution* gets away from Newport with 1O96, the 15.07 Saturdays-only Cardiff Central to Brighton service. 25 July 1987.

Tractor central at Cardiff as No. 37187 waits to depart westbound while a sister loco runs through with a freight train. 1979. (A. Gibbs)

Permissive working in action at Cardiff Central: as a London-bound HST set departs, a Class 118 DMU rolls into the occupied platform. Summer 1979. (A. Gibbs)

After the triple-headed Class 37 Llanwern–Port Talbot iron ore trains came the equally noisy double-headed Class 56 workings. Nos 56035 and 56037 pass through Cardiff en route to Port Talbot. July 1981. (A. Gibbs)

No. 37287 with an eastbound air-braked freight passes No. 33026 at Cardiff Central. 16 April 1982.

The reliable Class 33s were synonymous with the Cardiff to Portsmouth route, and in later years between Cardiff, Crewe and Manchester too. At Cardiff Central we find No. 33021 waiting to depart with 1O42, the 13.05 departure to Portsmouth Harbour. 17 September 1987.

Prior to the Class 33s, the Portsmouth route was the domain of the Class 31s. Though they were ousted from the Portsmouth to Bristol leg of the journey, they would still make occasional appearances further west. No. 31421 has just arrived at Bristol with a service from Portsmouth Harbour. July 1981. (A. Gibbs)

It's Peak power for 1V22, the 08.20 Brighton to Cardiff Central, with No. 45102 providing the traction on this day. 13 February 1982.

An interesting DMU combination at Cardiff Central with a pair of Gloucester-built Class 100 cars sandwiching a Class 101 trailer. While unnumbered, the Gloucester vehicles were Nos 51109 and 51110. 29 May 1982.

Originating in Portsmouth, No. 31187 has just arrived at Cardiff Central, having worked this train in from Bristol Temple Meads. 22 May 1982.

No. 33020 creeps around the back of Cardiff Canton depot with an ECS working, having just arrived from Portsmouth. Classes 31 and 37 can be seen on the depot. 28 October 1981.

Approaching Carmarthen station with 2C60, the 11.15 Swansea to Milford Haven, we find a grubby No. 37187 and its short rake of Mk 1 coaches. July 1981. (A. Gibbs)

In typical filthy WR condition, Tractor No. 37190 rolls into Whitland with a Milford Haven to Swansea service. July 1981. (A. Gibbs)

At Whitland station we find No. 37271 passing through with a train of oil tanks bound for Milford Haven.
A Class 120 DMU can be seen stabled in the bay platform. July 1981. (A. Gibbs)

The driver of No. 37180 *Sir Dyfed/County of Dyfed* chats to the booking clerk at Tenby while waiting
for the signal. The train in the adjacent platform was an ER set of coaches that worked to Tenby on the
Saturdays-only service from Hull. It was then utilised on local services to and from Swansea before returning
north the following weekend. July 1981. (A. Gibbs)

Trains pass at Tenby. On the left, No. 47441 has just terminated here with 1V74, the 08.29 Saturdays-only from Leeds, which had a portion from Hull attached at Sheffield. On the right is No. 47159, working 2B23, the 15.45 Saturdays-only Pembroke Dock to Swansea. This train had worked to Pembroke Dock earlier in the day on 1B22, the 10.07 Saturdays-only service from Paddington. 18 August 1984.

No. 37180 *Sir Dyfed/County of Dyfed* again. This locomotive appeared to haunt me on this holiday as I seemed to be riding behind it at least once a day. The loco is seen here approaching Tenby with a service to Swansea. July 1981. (A. Gibbs)

Crossing the golf links and sand dunes at Tenby is a Swindon-built Class 120 DMU set, illuminated by the setting sun. July 1981. (A. Gibbs)

Approaching Pembroke station is Swindon-built Class 120 cross-country DMU set No. 557, which is seen en route to Whitland. July 1981. (A. Gibbs)

The final image is at Johnston, in Pembrokeshire. No. 47318 waits to gain the single line towards Milford Haven or Waterston with a train of empty oil tanks. July 1981. (A. Gibbs)